Dai the Spy

Written by
Mignonne Gunasekara

Illustrated by
Emre Karacan

Chapter One

Dai's Dilemma

Dai felt sick.

He looked out at the sea of faces looking back at him and clutched his award a little tighter in his hands.

"Thank you all so much," said Dai. "This really is an honour."

A bead of sweat formed at his temple. Dai hoped his audience couldn't see it.

Dai the Spy

Spy

Level 10 – White

Helpful Hints for Reading at Home

The graphemes (written letters) and phonemes (units of sound) used throughout this series are aligned with Letters and Sounds. This offers a consistent approach to learning whether reading at home or in the classroom.

HERE ARE SOME COMMON WORDS THAT YOUR CHILD MIGHT FIND TRICKY:

water	where	would	know	thought	through	couldn't
laughed	eyes	once	we're	school	can't	our

TOP TIPS FOR HELPING YOUR CHILD TO READ:

- Encourage your child to read aloud as well as silently to themselves.
- Allow your child time to absorb the text and make comments.
- Ask simple questions about the text to assess understanding.
- Encourage your child to clarify the meaning of new vocabulary.

This book focuses on developing independence, fluency and comprehension. It is a white level 10 book band.

"But I am running out of room at home so this one is going in the downstairs toilet!" he joked. "Enjoy the rest of the night, everyone."
And with that, Dai slinked away. He was so glad that was over. The smiling and chatting he'd been doing all night had made him so tired.

Dai made his way home, but he still couldn't relax. He wasn't just nervous from speaking at the party. Dai felt like he was living a lie. He had an amazing reputation as the world's best spy, but he didn't feel like he deserved it.

Because Dai knew the truth. He wasn't a brilliant, skilled spy. He was just incredibly, incredibly lucky.

He had never failed a mission, but he had nothing but luck to thank for that. It always saved the day while Dai was nothing short of hopeless.

He walked over to the trophy cabinet in his living room.

BEST ANIMAL
RECAPTURED

BEST LUNCH
CHOICE

THE ROGER BARKMAN
AWARD EXCELLENCE IN ESPIONAGE

BEST FOILING
JEWELLERY HEIST

SPY
OF
THE
YEAR
2000

SPY
OF
THE
YEAR
2001

SPY
OF
THE
YEAR
2002

SPY
OF
THE
YEAR
2003

SPY
OF
THE
YEAR
2004

SPY
OF
THE
YEAR
2005

It was full. He had not been joking about that. There were trophies from throughout his career. They reminded Dai of all the times he'd barely done anything.

There was an award for the time Dai recovered some stolen jewels. The robbers had dropped them as they were running away and all Dai did was pick them up.

Another award was for when Dai 'rescued' a rare white t̶ had been stolen from the zoo. Dai h̶ about to leave to look for it when th̶ returned to the zoo by itself. It had e̶ e̶ from its captors on its own, but Dai g̶ l the credit.

Chance had got him all these awards, but Dai felt like his luck was running out now. He had decided to retire. It was only a matter of time before something went wrong on a mission that even luck couldn't fix. Dai didn't want to stick around to find out what that would be.

Suddenly, Dai's watch lit up. It was a message from The Boss.

Oh no. Dai hadn't told her about his retirement plans yet. This was awkward. He would have to tell her at the meeting. But it would probably be too late to find a replacement for him by then...

People were counting on him, and Dai didn't want to let them down. He decided to push his luck and take the mission on. After all, what was the worst that could happen?

Chapter Two

The Meeting

Dai met with The Boss at Headquarters the next morning. He was trying to act cool, but the worries at the back of his mind kept bubbling to the surface. If The Boss noticed, she didn't say anything. They went into her office and she pulled a case out from under her desk.

"Your task is simple, Agent X," she said. "There is a power plant, not far from here. You need to shut it down."

"It is dumping toxic waste into the ocean," said The Boss. "We cannot let them continue to cause such damage to the environment."

She clicked the case open and spun it around so Dai could see inside. There was a small device that looked like a remote control in there.

"A Zapper," she said. "It will freeze your enemy where they stand."

The Boss reached under her desk again and pulled out a pair of boots.

"These are magnetic boots," she continued. "You'll need them to get into the power plant. You will need to get into the control room and press the 'deactivate' button. That shuts everything down."

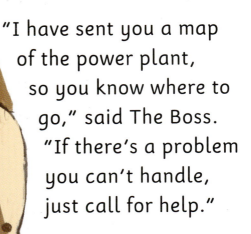

"I have sent you a map
of the power plant,
so you know where to
go," said The Boss.
"If there's a problem
you can't handle,
just call for help."

Dai picked up the
Zapper and put it
in his pocket.

"I'm ready," he said.
"I just have one question."

"What's that, Agent X?" asked
The Boss.

"I was wondering if this could be my final
mission."

"You want to retire?" asked The Boss.
Dai nodded.

"Of course, Agent X," said the Boss. "Complete this mission, and you can leave this world behind. If that's what you want."
"It is," replied Dai.

Chapter Three

The Power Plant

Dai stood outside the power plant. He had cut through the plant's fence and snuck past all their security cameras. All he had to do now was climb up the side of the building and get to the control room. Simple.

Dai made his way up to the third floor and pulled himself through a window. He was dusting himself off when he was spotted by a guard at the other end of the corridor.

"Hey!" yelled the guard as he charged towards Dai.

"Oh, crumbs," said Dai. He turned to run away but didn't get far before a loud thud made him turn around.

Dai couldn't believe what he was seeing. In his hurry to catch Dai, the guard had crashed into a closed glass door. It was part of a glass wall that stretched across the width of the corridor. Neither of them had spotted it, but the guard was now a human splat. He slowly slid to the floor. Dai decided to take advantage of this and get a head start.

"Sorry!" called Dai over his shoulder as he vanished around the corner. He felt bad for the guard, but he pushed it from his mind. The quicker he finished his mission and got out of there, the better.

Dai looked down at his watch as he ran. The map The Boss had sent him was on the screen. It said the control room was behind the next door in that corridor. Luckily the door was unlocked, so Dai let himself in.

However, Dai was not prepared for what he saw in the control room. In front of him was a huge control panel that wrapped around the room. Above it, screens of all different sizes were stacked up to the ceiling. Each screen was playing video footage of a different part of the power plant. Finding the 'deactivate' button was going to be tricky.

Dai got closer and saw that most of the buttons were labelled. Well, that made his job a lot easier. If there wasn't one labelled 'deactivate', maybe there was one labelled 'stop the toxic waste'. Dai was so busy reading all the labels that he didn't notice a guard enter the control room behind him.

"Aha!" exclaimed Dai. "That'll be the one."

He had found a big yellow button in the centre of the control panel. He leaned over to press it, but as he did so his Zapper fell out of his pocket. When it hit the floor, it fired at the incoming guard.

The guard was frozen in place before Dai even realised he was in the room.

Dai pushed the big yellow button and took a step back. His work here was done. He turned to leave and came face to face with the frozen guard.

"Ah!" Dai yelped. But before he could think about or do anything else, there was an almighty rumble. The whole building shook. Suddenly, an alarm started blaring. Dai turned back to the control panel. All the screens were flashing with the same warning message:

SELF-DESTRUCT ACTIVATED

Dai was so confused. He had pressed the 'deactivate' button, hadn't he?

Chapter Four

The Worst That Could Happen

He read the yellow button's label:

SELF-DESTRUCT

"They both have a 'd' in them," Dai said to the frozen guard. "It's an easy mistake to make... right?"

The guard couldn't reply. Dai ran out of the control room. The plant was going to blow – then all the waste would get released into the sea at once!

He had to do something, and fast. Dai scrambled outside, towards the waste tanks. In the background, the alarm was still blaring and all the staff were running towards the exits in a panic.

Before Dai could get to the tanks, he spotted a seal on the beach.

The tanks would empty right onto the poor animal. Dai was torn – should he save the seal, or keep going to the toxic waste tanks ahead?

Dai couldn't bring himself to leave the seal behind. He turned and ran towards it instead of the waste tanks, and scooped it up in his arms. Now he had to get out of the way of the toxic waste that was surely about to hit them both.

Behind him, the plant finally exploded. Dai hadn't managed to get out of the waste's path in time. Still clutching the seal, he fell to his knees and waited for the waste to flow over him.

Moments went by and nothing happened. Dai looked up to see the plant in ruins. Parts of it were on fire and smoke and dust were coming off it in clouds. But there was no overflowing toxic waste. Dai was confused. Still holding the seal, he made his way back.

He walked over to where the waste tanks were. They were broken... but they were also empty. Where had the waste gone?

Dai's question was answered when a charred piece of paper drifted down from the sky and landed on the seal's face. Dai picked it up. It had been damaged in the fire, but he could still read it.

Dai's eyes darted to his watch. It said that today was Tuesday. He slowly put the piece of paper in his pocket while trying not to make eye contact with the seal. It was silly, but Dai felt like the seal knew what was happening.

Just then, Dai heard the whirring of a helicopter. Sure enough, one appeared above him and dropped a rope ladder down to him. The Boss peered out of the helicopter's door. Dai moved the seal so he was holding it with one arm and used his other to grab hold of the ladder. He began to climb it as the helicopter started to fly away.

Dai and the seal were buckled up inside the helicopter when The Boss spoke.

"Well done, Agent X," she said. "That was a little messy, but it got the job done. You are now free to retire."

Dai breathed a sigh of relief. He'd had enough luck left in him to pull off one last mission.

The Boss dropped Dai and the seal off at Dai's house. The seal gave Dai a disappointed look, then shuffled away. Dai was grateful that seals couldn't talk.

He went inside and sat down in his office.
It was all over. Dai took the piece of paper out of his pocket... and shredded it.

Dai the Spy

1. Where did Dai joke about putting his new award?

2. What animal did Dai have to rescue after it was stolen from the zoo?

3. Where did Dai meet The Boss?

   (a) At Headquarters

   (b) At a restaurant

   (c) At a bus stop

4. What gadgets did The Boss give Dai?

5. Have you ever been in a difficult situation like Dai? How did you get out of it?

©2021 **BookLife Publishing Ltd.**
King's Lynn, Norfolk PE30 4LS

ISBN 978-1-83927-437-4

Dai the Spy
Written by Mignonne Gunasekara
Illustrated by Emre Karacan

An Introduction to BookLife Readers...

Our Readers have been specifically created in line with the London Institute of Education's approach to book banding and are phonetically decodable and ordered to support each phase of Letters and Sounds.

Each book has been created to provide the best possible reading and learning experience. Our aim is to share our love of books with children, providing both emerging readers and prolific page-turners with beautiful books that are guaranteed to provoke interest and learning, regardless of ability.

BOOK BAND GRADED using the Institute of Education's approach to levelling.

PHONETICALLY DECODABLE supporting each phase of Letters and Sounds.

EXERCISES AND QUESTIONS to offer reinforcement and to ascertain comprehension.

BEAUTIFULLY ILLUSTRATED to inspire and provoke engagement, providing a variety of styles for the reader to enjoy whilst reading through the series.

AUTHOR INSIGHT: MIGNONNE GUNASEKARA

Despite being BookLife Publishing's newest recruit, Mignonne Gunasekara has already written fourteen books about everything from starter science and disastrous deaths throughout history to dinosaurs.

Born in Sri Lanka, Mignonne has always been drawn to stories, whether they are told through literature, film or music. After studying Biomedical Science at King's College London, Mignonne completed a short course in screenwriting at the National Centre for Writing in Norwich, during which she explored writing scripts for the different mediums of film, theatre and radio.

This book focuses on developing independence, fluency and comprehension. It is a white level 10 book band.